A Child Cries

The Pain of Searching *For Love*

JACQUELINE BONNER SINCLAIR

Published by Victorious You Press™
Charlotte NC, USA

Copyright © 2022 JACQUELINE BONNER SINCLAIR All rights reserved.

No part of this book may be reproduced, distributed or transmitted in any form by any means, graphic, electronic, or mechanical, including photocopy, recording, taping, or by any information storage or retrieval system, without permission in writing from the author except in the case of reprints in the context of reviews, quotes, or references.

While the author has made every effort to ensure that the ideas, statistics, and information presented in this Book are accurate to the best of his/her abilities, any implications direct, derived, or perceived, should only be used at the reader's discretion. The author cannot be held responsible for any personal or commercial damage arising from communication, application, or misinterpretation of the information presented herein.

Unless otherwise indicated, scripture quotations are from the Holy Bible, King James Version. All rights reserved.

TITLE: A CHILD CRIES
First Printed: September 2022
Cover Designer: NADIA MONSANO
ISBN: 978-1-952756-87-0

Printed in the United States of America

For details email joan@victoriousyoupress.com
or visit us at www.victoriousyoupress.com

Dedication

This book is dedicated to women who have suffered abuse and kept it silent for a lifetime. It is also for those who have found the courage to forgive, move on, and thrive.

Acknowledgements

Heartfelt thanks to Josephine Simpson, Fitzalva Sinclair, Yvonne Shirley, Alicia Maxwell, Mr. Wayne Robinson, Nolalee Rodney, and my two adorable children: Taneka Morris and Richard Stephenson, for their unquantifiable love and support in making this project a reality.

Table Of Contents

Introduction 1
1. A Child In Need 3
2. Betrayal 11
3. Growing Up 21
4. Church Girls 31
5. Change Came 37
6. Sadness 47
7. Pain And More Pain 51
8. I Have A Winning Faith 55
9. Finding Mom 67
10. Sisterly Love 81
11. Words That Comforted Me 95
12. The Man, Noel 99
13. New Chapter 107

Introduction

This book is the result of many tears and prayers. It was born out of empathy for victims of rape, abuse, rejection, heartache, grief, and abandonment. It is intended to encourage and inspire individuals who have lived a challenging life and feel there is no more hope for them and those who think their lives have no meaning.

Jesus used the teaching power of stories through parables to bless others; indeed, the story of my life unfolds like a parable. I pray that as I share some of the episodes of my life that you will find value and purpose in your life and see how God is our redeeming friend.

I have survived an onslaught of crises that would kill or drive an ordinary person insane. I have experienced the horrors of child abuse, rape, teenage pregnancy, abandonment, unemployment, homelessness, domestic abuse, medical issues, and other adversities. I can vividly recall a point in my life when I couldn't eat because there was no food; I had no place to sleep, and those memories still haunt me with each passing day.

I was abused by men that were supposed to love and care for me as a child. I felt rejected by my mother, who I believed loved her significant other more than she loved me. I often wondered what I had done to deserve such loathing and despair as a child. Why was my life so difficult? Why was I neglected? What excluded me from being worthy of parental love like my other siblings?

This book is dedicated to any woman who is a victim of life, especially those who have suffered rape. Sometimes, the babies conceived and born during those unfortunate circumstances don't receive the love and affection they need. If you have ever been there or found yourself in this position, I pray that you will find comfort in the arms of the Lord. He knows your address. He knows you, and he has a definite plan and purpose for your life and your child's life.

In the process of writing this book, I experienced a shift. I held onto my pain for many years and carried the burdens in my heart for decades, but as my fingers wrote my story, my spirit became alive, and I felt a release. My prayer is that my story will help you to release the burden you may be carrying in your heart.

Chapter 1

A Child In Need

I attempted to end my life because of my unwanted pregnancy.

My friend's brother raped me. He believed that I was not supposed to sleep in his house without sleeping with him. I was pregnant at age sixteen as a result and ended up living on the streets of Kingston, Jamaica. I went from house to house, trying to find shelter with friends, family, or anyone who would accept me in their home.

As a child, I had spent several years seeking refuge from my abusive stepfather, who threw me out of his house whenever he physically abused my mom because I would try to defend her. For a time, I stayed with my uncle, who I believed loved and cared for me as his niece, but he didn't. He turned out to be just as deceitful as my friend's brother. He preyed on my vulnerability and molested me when I sought refuge at his house. He betrayed my trust, and, in turn, I nurtured a hatred for him that poisoned my soul.

My life felt empty, partly because I was raised in a household without affection and compassion. I didn't receive validation from the people closest to me who were supposed to love me. Growing up, I was an introvert with low self-esteem, which I cite as a consequence of being constantly exploited, undermined, and mistreated. I was drowning deep in an abyss of "I am not good enough."

My name is Jacqueline Bonner Sinclair. I was born in Kingston, Jamaica. I am the second child of Josephine and Donald Bonner (the sperm donor), who didn't accept me as his child because his mother told him that I was too dark-complexioned and not as light-skinned as he was. What a joke! While growing up, I couldn't understand why she said I was not his child because of my skin complexion when both my parents were black. When I think back, my father's brother, who shared the same parents, was as dark-complexioned as I am.

My mother was a beautiful woman who was pleasing to the eye and had a warm personality. She was the youngest of seven children. My grandfather had passed away and left my grandmother with all seven children to care for single-handedly. My grandma had big hopes for my mother, who she thought was brilliant and had excellent prospects. One day, my handsome father swept my beautiful mother off her feet. My mom was in college but dropped out because she started having children with him. By the time my mother was nineteen, they already had two children. Later, my mom found out that he had a secret child. Two months before I was born, a woman had given birth to a baby boy who he sired. So, my mom left my dad.

At the age of twenty, my mother met another man. She thought he would love her and her two daughters more than the man she had left. It didn't take her long to discover that he was only a philanderer and had also dated all the women at his job. Then, at twenty-one, she met Ruggles (that is what we called him). He was charming and handsome, so no one could blame her for falling for him. Shortly after meeting him, she got pregnant with his child. Hence my mom decided to move in with him. THAT WAS A MISTAKE!

My mother's hope of securing a home filled with love and joy dissipated as she realized that this new home with Ruggles as the head was riddled with all types of abuse. Ruggles was an extremely insecure and jealous man filled with rage and fury. He controlled my mother and. wouldn't let her go out or see family and friends. She had no way to seek help. He was a master of tyranny and used fear as a weapon of control.

After my mom gave birth to his first child, the abuse intensified. My mother became his punching bag. Their physical fights spiraled out of control and got louder and more dangerous by the days. Soon, I became a target and would receive a good whipping every time they fought. I tried desperately to protect my mom, but he would push me out of the way and let me pay for my brazen attempts to be her hero. He would tell me to leave and look for my father and declared that he was not looking after any man's child. That became his tagline. Those words would pierce my young soul, and I would always cry. Sometimes, I cried for hours to the point where I was nicknamed "Cry Cry."

Ruggles made sure my mother couldn't seek external help or escape his abusive control by getting her pregnant. When she got pregnant the second time, he accused her of trying to leave, to which she responded, "Where am I going with my children, and there is another on the way?" The road to destruction had just begun.

After the birth of his second child, Ruggles calmed down. He did so because my mom had decided she would leave him if he didn't stop beating her. He agreed to stop, and things were peaceful. It didn't last, though, as my mom got pregnant once more, and the fighting started all over again. My mom left and took us to the country, where we were safe in the shelter and security of family members. Ruggles came crying and begged her to return with him, and she obliged. He was peaceful and pleasant for a short period before he returned to his typical ways. Ruggles strengthened his strategy of power and control when my mother returned to him. He moved us farther and farther away from our family and friends. He told my mom that he didn't want anyone at his house. When a family member came to visit, he humiliated and disparaged them. He also ensured my mom couldn't hold down a job since we moved so frequently.

I remember when we moved to a place called "Mosquito Valley." At the time, it was a newly developed housing scheme deep in the woods of Red Hills. One day, my mom went into labor and was admitted to the hospital. The following day, this abusive man brought a woman to the house and told us she was there to do the cleaning and cooking. I noticed she didn't do any of the chores he claimed she came there to do. He ensured that we went to school earlier than usual, without lunch or lunch money. He lied and told us he would take lunch for us at school, but he never did.

A Child Cries

One day, I decided to hide in the house and let him think I had gone to school. I saw the woman come to the house, and he invited her in and locked the door. I confronted her when she finished her 'task' and was about to leave. I didn't know that my voice would resonate for Ruggles to hear me from where he was. I was, in fact, shouting at this home-wrecker. I decided to throw stones at her for coming to our home, disrespecting my mother's house, sleeping with her husband, and having the nerve to do it around children. She thought we were clueless and didn't understand what was happening. Ruggles decided he would beat me because, in his estimation, I was rude and out of order to confront his woman. I told him I was going to tell my mom. He ran after me, and I ran for my life. I wasn't going to take another beating from him.

I walked from Red Hills to Kingston Jubilee Hospital (approximately 20 miles) to tell my mom. I couldn't return to that house, so I spent the night at my aunt's home. My aunt told me I would have to go back home in the morning because she did not have enough space to accommodate me. I couldn't return to that house because Ruggles had declared that he would kill me.

We never had much food or nice clothes to wear, and I had walked the 20 miles barefooted! Still, I had to return to this life of lack and abuse even though my life was in jeopardy. I sat on a little far-off rock when I returned to the complex. I must have looked weary and dejected. A man named Mr. Johnson approached me and enquired about my wellbeing. He worked for "Best Dress Chicken" as one of the chief executive officers. He became my savior. When I didn't have food, he brought me groceries. I hid them from Ruggles and brought them to my mom to feed us. I will never forget the people who helped me in my time of struggles and despair. May God bless them and their family.

Chapter 2

Betrayal

After the Red Hills incident, we moved back to Kingston. I was happy to be close to some of my family again. They couldn't do much for us, but the thought of being near them brought some level of hope.

The move wasn't the only change. We started to notice a shift in my stepfather's behavior as well. He came home later than usual and left the house abruptly on occasions, saying that he was going to see a friend in Salt Lane (a known bad place). My mom found out that he was seeing another woman. She was pregnant with a baby girl, and that was the reason for his change—he was distracted. After my mom discovered the pregnancy, the abuse started again. He didn't want her to say anything to anyone, and he often accused me of being the problem to deflect from his philandering. He blamed me for the trouble in the house.

We were close to family, but my mom still didn't have anywhere to escape. I became the house helper since I was the oldest and had to do everything by myself. I was about eight at the time. My grandmother took my older sister Jasmine. My grandmother preferred Jasmine because she had a fairer complexion than I did. She only loved Jasmine and other light-skinned people. If you were too dark-skinned like me, she wanted no association with you. Back then, I had little to no understanding of the prejudice associated with dark-complexioned people, but I was old enough to know that I was not liked.

So, I had no place but to stay with my mother and stepfather. I had to endure the brutal beatings and struggles. Sometimes, I didn't go to school because I didn't have shoes, lunch money, or bus fare. But when I was allowed to attend school, it was my haven. Back then, I went to school regularly without food. It was the norm for me. However, once I was not at the house, I was good.

I never played around at school; I sat in class and behaved responsibly. I wouldn't leave class during lunch. I stayed there and did my schoolwork. I didn't know that there was a teacher who noticed that I never left class during the lunch period. She noted how long I sat in the class and noticed that I never went outside to play, eat, or take breaks like everyone else. Her name was Miss Gray. God bless her soul! One day, she called me to her desk and asked, "Why do you never leave the class to take your lunch break?" I lied and told her that it was because I wasn't hungry.

I went to school barefooted. My mom wasn't allowed to buy anything for me using my stepdad's money, so whenever my grandmother traveled overseas, she would bring things for me. Sometimes, I would take my mom's shoes. They were much smaller, but I would break down the backs to accommodate my bigger feet. I did this so the asphalt wouldn't burn my feet on hot days.

I don't remember at what point, but I learned to pray early. I asked God to send someone to my rescue. The first verse I remember learning is Psalm 6:2-3, "Have mercy on me, O Lord, for I *am* weak; O Lord, heal me, for my bones are troubled. My soul also is greatly troubled; But You, O Lord—how long?" (NKJV). I'm not sure if that was the first verse I read, but reading it felt good because I was at a place of weakness, trembling, and depression. I felt like David. I could confess to God exactly how I felt. I was weary from crying and sleeping on a wet pillow every night.

One day, the teacher, Miss Gray, told me she had signed me up for lunch at the canteen. I was speechless and numb. Overwhelmed with emotion, I cried, and she just hugged me like a loving mother. I wanted to feel the touch of my birth mother, but there was nothing that she could do to comfort me in the times of my pain and hurt. I then started sharing my traumas with Miss Gray. My situation moved her heart, and she started giving me bus fare for school. God sent me an angel to lighten a little girl's burden and carried me through the dark tunnels of my childhood.

I remember one Friday evening so clearly. My stepfather came home, and all of us girls were sitting on the porch at our new home on Chelsea Avenue in New Kingston. This upscale community saw me through a new level in my life. My stepfather said something about a cup. I didn't realize that he was talking to me. He walked up to me and said, "You are the older one; why is the cup there?" I didn't know how to respond because I didn't understand what he was talking about. He got angry, slapped me in the face, and began berating me, "So you think you are a big woman!"

I am thirteen, I said to myself. Then I looked at him and said, "Today is going to be the last day; I am not taking any more abuse from you." I slapped him back, and this ignited a war between us. I took off, and he ran after me,

Betrayal

yelling, "You are not staying in this house!" I screamed, "As long as my mother is in this house, I am staying!"

What happened next scared the life out of me. He locked me out of the house and told me he would not give me food. My sisters sneaked and opened the door allowing me entry later in the night, but I got caught. He said, "So, you are a big woman? Now, I will do what big people do to you." He stuck his tongue in my mouth. I grabbed it with my teeth and bit down on it. When I released him, I had blood in my mouth. I ran out of the house and headed to the Halfway Tree Police Station a few miles away for help. After they took my report, they took me back to the house. I knew in my heart that nothing good would come of this. When we arrived, he told them that I was "bad." "Bad" is the simple term used to describe an uncontrollable Jamaican child. He told them we were having a conversation when I jumped up and bit him, then ran off. They believed his story and left.

After they were gone, he put what little clothing I had in a paper bag and threw it in the middle of the street. There was an open lot in the back of the property, so I picked up my bag and sat in the empty lot out of the view of passersby. I didn't want anyone to see me there crying.

A Child Cries

My mom was hurt because I didn't obey his order, but she tried to speak in my defense. He slapped her face before I ran from the house when she did this. He shouted at her, "She's not coming into this house. Let her leave my place."

Mom couldn't help me, and all I could do was cry. She was afraid of this man and what he would do to her. I was fearful for her all the time. I stayed outside for as long as possible and then begged him to let me back in. He refused. I called out to my mom to save me from sleeping out in the street, but all she said was, "Please, find somewhere and go!"

It was very late as night had fallen a while ago. Where was I supposed to go? I picked up some stones nearby and said, "If I am not sleeping in this house, no one else is going to sleep." I threw the rocks over the fence until I broke all the house windows. He called the police, but I ran and hid before they came. I watched, waited for them to leave, and threw more stones at the house. I slept in the bushes in the open lot that night.

When morning came, I waited for him to leave and went back to the house so that I could take a shower and grab something to eat. My mom's face was all black and blue from the beating she took for my disobedience. I blamed myself. I felt like everything that happened to my

Betrayal

mom was because of me. I was an unwanted problem child.

A few days after wandering around and sleeping in the open lot, I snuck back into the house and hid from him. I slept for a couple of days under the bed and was stealthy during the days. One day, he found out that I was in the house. He decided he would whip all my siblings if they didn't tell him where I was hiding in the house. My conscience wouldn't permit them to suffer on my behalf, so I stepped forward. I told him, "I am not afraid of you. I am not leaving because my mom is in this house." He said, "Okay. I am going to beat you like how they beat a whore." He went outside and pulled the hose from the garden and told me that he would beat me with it. He grabbed me, and I grabbed him back. He had dreadlocks, so I wrapped my hands in his hair. I decided I was not letting him go because holding his hair would weaken him! We fought until his friend stopped by and broke it up. He insisted that I had to leave his house. At this point, I knew I had no choice but to go to my uncle's house that night to stay.

That was another big mistake.

My uncle—my favorite uncle—molested me while I was going through my darkest moment. I didn't tell anyone because he threatened and warned me not to.

I found another Bible verse that comforted me in my lonely hours. Psalm 13:1-2, "How long, O Lord? Will You Forget Me forever? How long will You hide Your face from me? How long shall I take counsel in my soul, Having sorrow in my heart daily? How long will my enemy be exalted over me?" (NKJV).

My question was, how long? There is profound torture in not knowing how long an ordeal will last. Till tomorrow? Next week? Next year? The rest of my life? It is the unknown that makes it so hard to bear.

After I left, my stepfather sold the house and moved. Now, I had no access to my mother and siblings. My mom had no say in his decisions. She knew I would not be able to live with them permanently, so she kept telling me to find someplace to live where I could be safe. She was tired of seeing me crying and in pain, but she couldn't help or prevent him from beating me. She couldn't help herself even from being battered by him. I asked myself, *why would a mother choose a man over her child?* I was broken and lost. I had no clothes, no money, and no sense of direction. I needed my mother to love me enough to want me. I decided to go to the countryside and live with my maternal grandmother. She lived in the Portland parish, about sixty miles away from my uncle's house, on the rural east coast of the Island.

Betrayal

As a young girl, I loved going to the countryside of Portland to spend time with my grandmother and other family members during summer breaks. I would always take the bus. The bus stop was right in front of my grandmother's house. I loved seeing and talking with the female conductor, Ms. Millie because she knew my grandmother well. It was always a happy time to visit the country.

I went to the bus station hoping to see Miss Millie so I could tell her that I wanted to go to my grandmother's house, but I had no money. I got on her bus, explained to her that I was going to live with my grandmother, and told her everything that had happened. Miss Millie hugged me and told me to sit beside her. I smiled as I did. In the back of my mind, I was worried about what my grandmother would say. But after taking my seat, I quickly fell asleep. I woke up when we got to Buff Bay, about fifteen miles from my destination. Miss Millie offered me something to eat. I was grateful because I was famished.

When we reached my location, Miss Millie called out to my grandmother. She said, "I have your granddaughter here." My grandmother thanked her. I got off, and as soon as the bus left, she asked the questions I was afraid of: "Why are you here? Where's your mom?" After I answered, she expressed that she was too old to look after me and couldn't afford to. She also said she didn't want me to get pregnant while living at her house. My heart was sad and broken, but I had to be brave for myself. I stayed. I went from a city girl to a country girl. Everything had changed in moments. I had to learn the country life fast and how to fend for myself. I would have to learn how to harvest bananas, dig yam ridges, pick oranges, and acquire just about any food provisions to sell so that I could provide for the household. I still had to finish school, even though it was far away, and I had to walk. My old life as a broken, bitter town girl had shifted to a new experience as a country girl. I had to learn quickly to shift gears from brokenness to survival mode. This time was the happiest of my teenage years.

Chapter 3

Growing Up

On my sixteenth birthday, my grandmother called me into her room and said, "Today, you are a woman. I no longer want you here, so you must return to your mother. I can't look after you anymore because you're turning into a woman, and life is changing. I don't want you to stay in the country. I don't want anything to happen to you here, and I am held responsible, so I am sending you back home to your mother." While tears poured down my cheeks, I told her I would be fine living with her.

My heart was re-broken and torn into shreds. I didn't know how to stop the pain, and I

couldn't sleep for days. I ran away to my great aunt's house. I tried to plead with them to coerce my grandma to let me stay. They told me they had no say in the matter; hence I had to go back to Kingston. That's what my grandmother said, so that is what will be. "Can I Stay with you then?" I asked. My great aunt said, "No." I gave up. My short-lived happiness had turned into sadness and pain. Every terrible moment I experienced at my stepfather's house haunted me. I was overwhelmed with the traumatic memories and knew what would happen. While on the bus, I couldn't help the tears that flowed to Kingston.

I arrived at the house and was greeted with my stepfather's unwelcome but familiar words. "You are not staying here. Go look for your father." Usually, he would also give me about two or three different names of my possible fathers. Any man he thought of that used to like or love my mom or any man he thought had ever looked at her from a distance would be named as my father. My mother was quiet while he spoke. She didn't want to make him upset and start a fight. When he was done, she said, "Jackie, go put your things in the room with your sisters."

The first two days were surprisingly good until it dawned on him that I was back in the

house. This realization seemed to release his demons as he went out of his way to find something he thought I should be doing. He ensured that I never got a break or have a carefree play day with my sisters and brothers. I had to do everything. My sisters were excused from doing any chore or task because they were his children. I told myself, *here it goes again. The same ordeal all over again. I am back as the slave girl.* He ensured that my life was miserable and uncomfortable. My mother was now more afraid of him because she didn't know when he would find something to fuss or pick a fight about. It was as if she was walking in a mine field.

My mom's body was damaged in many ways by my stepfather. He ensured she never appeared or looked outside the house when his friends came by. My mom is a very attractive lady, but he made sure no one noticed her by impregnating her frequently. She would always look exhausted during and after pregnancy. He wanted to keep her in the background. But despite the damage, my mom's smile was worth dying for. You would have never known anything was going

on with her because her smile masked her pain very well, and she was also good at hiding the bruises. My mom wouldn't leave him, and I still didn't understand why. In her words, "I can't leave my children." She couldn't endure the gossip and whispering from our family, nor the discomfort and shame of leaving her children. She resigned to a life of battering and refused to go, but in my mind, I was saying, *Leave, Mom*!

A Child Cries

My stepfather had a furniture making business, and his clients were rich and famous people in Jamaica, like the prime minister and his associates. His business reputation probably made it hard for him to be seen as a bad person by his friends. He would beat her if she ever showed herself because he thought she only revealed herself to be noticed by the men who did business with him. All these businessmen weren't interested in my mom; however, her friendly personality would attract them to ask her about her children.

Back then, my brothers wore dreadlocks and were home-schooled by my mom, while my sisters and I went to school. My mom was smart. She was the brains behind my stepfather's business and was the one who took care of the paperwork. She was the brains, and he was the brawn as he only knew about the woodwork.

One day, he asked, "You think you are better than my children?" On this day, he asked me to wash all my siblings' clothes, and I refused. We were all grown up, and they could wash their clothes. He slapped me, and I returned the blow. We started our first big fight since I returned. He told me his favorite words, "Leave my house." I replied, "I am not leaving." He eventually pulled me out of the compound and locked the gate. It was about 1:30 am. I went to my aunt's home since he insisted that I leave. I wasn't going to stand outside the gate all night. I

thought my aunt would understand and accommodate me because all my family knew about the abusive situation at my house. My aunt refused to let me in her house. She said, "If your mother let you leave at this time of the night, why should I let you in mine?" I was so hurt and disappointed by her actions. I decided to hide in the flowers on her porch. I was so scared of being seen because the area she lived in was considered a dangerous area. God protected me that night, but the devil also had a plan for me.

My friend lived just down the road from my aunt's house. I decided to go and visit her and see if I could stay at her house for the night. She agreed to let me stay. This was the beginning of my sorrow. She escorted me to a room and said I could sleep there. I was asleep, and, to my horror and disbelief, her brother found out I was sleeping in the room and came hunting for fresh meat. He felt I couldn't sleep in his house without him sleeping with me. I fought for my life with no help!

The unforgivable happened—I was raped. When I saw all the blood and felt the pain. I knew I had lost my virginity to someone I didn't want to be with. I washed myself up and cried all day. I didn't have anyone to tell or to talk to; I was at the mercy of God. I got up, cleaned myself off, and tried to put on a brave face. I told myself I would put it behind me and find another place to stay. I was going through all this because of that evil man who threw me out and left me to the elements. There was no one to comfort or avenge me. I felt like nobody's child.

After my rape, I was homeless, constantly trying to find a place to lay my head. I couldn't go back to my stepfather's house. I attempted going back several times, but he would chase me away whenever I got to the gate. My sisters sneaked me in some nights and hid me under the bed. Other times, I would have to climb the mango tree and sit in it until he left. During my homelessness, I didn't know I was pregnant. My body was changing, and I kept having these bad feelings. I didn't know what was happening to me. Eventually, I went to my mom when he was not home. He came back, but we were unaware of his return. He overheard me explaining to my mom about the changes and how I felt in my body. I didn't tell her that I was raped. He stormed in and yelled at me, "That's what you wanted. Get out of my house, and don't corrupt my daughters."

I cried for days. The very thing my grandmother was trying to prevent from happening, happened to me. I was motherless and fatherless. I was in a bad spot and didn't know what to do. I hated him more than before because this wouldn't have happened if he hadn't locked me out late that night. He never cared for my mom, and he hated me. She was just a house helper, a punching bag, and a baby machine to him, getting pregnant every six or seven months.

I found out that my mom was pregnant with his seventh child. My mom and I were pregnant at the same time, only a few months apart. I felt alone. I cried and cried until there were no more tears left. I went to see my grandmother and told her about my ordeal, and she listened. She went with me to see the boy's mother, who lived in the same house where I was raped. It was a painful experience for me.

After my grandmother talked with his mother, they decided I could stay at the house until the baby was born. I had no choice because I had nowhere else to live. While I lived there, he decided I was now his 'baby mama.' I told him I was no one's 'baby mama' and that he better not call me that again! We argued all the time because he wanted me to be his girlfriend and 'baby mama,' and that certainly wasn't going to happen. It wasn't very easy for me to live there. I even tried to kill myself because of the unimaginable pain that I was going through. I was sixteen and unable to provide for myself. I was forced to depend on his mom since I was in her custody and care. I stayed there until the baby was born. I was depressed but didn't know that it was depression because back then, I had no idea what depression was. Instead, I just endured the pain and cried.

After my baby was born, the depression worsened, and all I knew was tears. I bathed in it day and night. My child's father and I constantly argued because he would not get his way. He remarked that I couldn't stay in his house or speak to him. My cousin lived on the other side of the house with his family. I asked him if I could stay there with them. He agreed but said he didn't have a bed for me to sleep in. I told him it was okay; I would sleep on the floor. I moved my stuff from my daughter's family's house and made myself comfortable in my cousin's home.

My child's father decided that his child couldn't leave with me. I spoke to his mom about the situation, and she resolved that the baby would alternate sleeping at their house and my cousin's house with me. I would get her early in the morning, then take her back at night. One night after I dropped her off, my child's father decided he would kill me if I didn't come back to his house and be with him. He held my neck and squeezed it mercilessly. God gave me the strength to reach for a flowerpot on the patio and knock him over his head. My cousin heard the noise, rushed out, and saw that he was trying to kill me. He saved me that night.

Growing Up

My baby turned two, but she still wouldn't eat or drink the regular food made for babies. All she wanted was breast milk, but my nipples were sore from feeding her. I had to find a way to wean her. I also had to find a way to distance myself from her father because living in the same area with the men I despised was unbearable.

I was on my own. I had no one to guide me. I had no work experience, but I went job hunting. I walked into a furniture store called "Courts. The store associate who greeted me asked, "How can I help you?" I told him that I was looking for a job. He asked if I could do sales. I didn't know what he was talking about. I laughed and proudly said, "No." He said he couldn't help me because they were looking for sales associates. I was heartbroken. I felt lost and hopeless. I cried out loud to God, "What sin have I committed? Lord, help me, please." But

God had set me up. He had a plan for me. He had a "ram in the thicket." He sent an angel in the form of a man to help me, right there in the store.

The store associate had walked away and left me standing in the same spot. Heavy

tears rolled down my face. This man came up to me and said, "Don't cry." I looked at him, my sorrow evident on my face. He wiped away my tears and introduced himself as Mr. Bryan. He was a short man with a disability. He explained that he and his partner had just opened a store next to Courts and they were looking for sales associates. He offered to employ and train me. The store was called "Winston's Furniture." That was my first job. A real job that wasn't housework. God had come through for me.

Chapter 4

Church Girls

While I was still staying with my child's family, I started searching for answers, but I wasn't getting any. There were many moments when I considered taking my life, but God comforted and consoled me in my lonely hours. I could hear him whispering in my ears, "I am with you."

One morning, I remember walking with the usual tears streaming down my face. I was thinking, *Lord, what will you do?* Out of nowhere, I heard a woman's voice say, "Good morning. Can we pray for you?" In front of me stood three young ladies. I could tell they were young Christian ladies living for the Lord by their clothes. I was taken aback by their question. I didn't know what to say, so I nodded. The older-looking young lady came up to me and introduced herself as Sarah. She said, "There's nothing too hard that God cannot fix." I had no doubt they God sent them to minister to me. They prayed for me, then all three of them hugged me. Sarah asked if they could give me a Bible study, and I accepted. I found out that they lived close by. We kept in touch and later became friends.

They shared the Word of God with me daily. The Word of God was my comfort when dark clouds arose. One day, they invited me to church. Their church was hosting a youth convention at the national stadium. I thought about my living situation and told them I couldn't attend. Every day they would say, "Now is the acceptable time. Jesus will fix it if you put it all in His hands." We were friends, but I still didn't mention my circumstances to them. I learned to hide things inside, just like my mother.

On the last day of the youth convention service, Janice, one of the young ladies, came looking for me. She said, "Today is your day." I told her then that I didn't have a place of my own, and I didn't know if my custodians would take issue if I gave my life to God. At this point, I couldn't allow anything to jeopardize my relationship with my cousin and possibly leave me homeless on the streets again. She prayed with me and said, "All is well."

My next issue was that I didn't have clothes for church. When I expressed this to her, she said, "I can fix that." I went to ask my cousin if I could go to church, and he gave me the go-ahead. I went to church, and it was a life-changing experience for me. That day, I got filled with the Holy Ghost.

I was still at the same house, going through the same pain, with the same folks, but something had changed. I prayed more earnestly and asked the Lord to guide and show me the way out. I started going to that church three times per week. I also read and studied the Word of God consistently. This led me to discover another favorite Scripture of mine. I was drawn to Isaiah 40:29, "He gives power to the weak, and to those who have no might He increases strength." (NKJV). It encouraged my heart greatly. I realized how important the process was. I then stopped resisting the uncomfortable moments in my life and embraced my future hopes. Yet, I was still thinking about my life and what I needed to do to escape the pain in my heart. My new sisters, Sarah, Janice, and Saudia started praying with me more often because I was still discouraged and upset over my situation.

The Words of God helped me to carry on with my daily duties of mothering and church while I worked. I decided I needed to stop going to my daughter's father's house. I had made up my mind about it. It was time for me to take flight, but I couldn't bring my daughter with me since I had no place of my own. I talked with his mom,

Miss Morgan, and her daughter Miss Paulette. Miss Morgan was a pastry chef, who worked for some high-profile people, and she told me that she would be moving to Portland to live and work. She said that she would take my three-year-old daughter with her. She said, "Jackie, go find life. I will help you and take care of my granddaughter, and you are free to check up on her anytime." I promised her that I wanted to keep my child but was unable at the time and that I would come to visit them as often as I could.

In all my time there, I grew to love Miss Morgan. I loved her for who she was and what she stood for. She prayed many times for me and encouraged me when she saw how sad I was. She also apologized on many occasions for her son's behavior and assured me that she would do whatever she could to assist me. She became a mother figure to me. When I couldn't visit her and my daughter, she updated me on what was happening and checked me regularly. She talked to me like my mother and encouraged me to make the necessary changes to better my life.

God was bringing new things into my life. At the time, I remember Proverbs 3:5-6, "Trust in the Lord with all your heart. And lean not on your understanding; In all your ways acknowledge Him, And He shall direct your paths." God worked out that situation for me right on time. I believed in his Words that He would make way for me somehow.

Chapter 5

Change Came

I decided to join the Jamaica Defense Force (JDF) to become an independent woman and the woman God wanted me to be. I went to Mr. Bryan seeking advice, and he assisted with the paperwork, extended himself to help me prepare for the exam, and encouraged me never to give up. Unfortunately, I had to lie to secure admission into the army. I couldn't tell them I had a child because I wouldn't be considered for enlistment if I did. Again, God hid me in His arms and protected me. My church was against a woman wearing pants. The pastor told me that the Jamaica Defense Force wasn't a place for me to be because it was a man's job. With a bright smile, I walked away from that church. I kept my beliefs, principles, and prayer life, and my sisters stood by my side.

I understood that a man didn't think a woman should be in the work field or advance in life higher than them. They also considered my profession to be masculine. For them, a woman's place was in the house, taking care of children and the home. They got that part wrong in my book. I had watched my mom do that all her life and saw what had dished her. I was not falling into that trap. I was determined and made a firm decision not to change paths. My life would be what I want it to be. I would stand strong for my children, and a man would not determine what my life would be.

The training camp was brutal. I didn't know how badly I would need God in my life. My Sargent picked on me constantly. He teased me and said I should return home because this was not a woman's job. Training camp was the place that tested my faith and strength. God kept my mind from going crazy. Looking back, I realize that place strengthened me emotionally, spiritually, and psychologically. I had to pray earnestly for the strength to carry on. I made it through victoriously. I didn't see my daughter for several months because of training but graduating made it worth it. I could finally live out my dreams with her, which strengthened my resolve to succeed even more.

I decided to live on-site as a young caddy; that's what we were called back then. I prayed daily for God to keep my mind in the right place and my child safe. My prayer life became a daily comfort to me. My sisters and the church folks would also encourage me. My sisters would say, "Hold to God with unchanging hands. He will keep you." I was able to study the Bible again since training was over. Here are some Scripture verses that comforted me as I read and understood the Word of God for myself.

Psalm 34:18, "The Lord is near to those who have a broken heart, And saves such as have a contrite spirit." (NKJV). Psalm 23:4, "Yea, though I walk through the valley of the shadow of death, I will fear no evil; For You are with me; Your rod and Your staff, they comfort me." (NKJV).

Those words are the promises from God's heart to comfort mine. Since I had finished training, I was able to visit my daughter. It was difficult bonding and showing her love. I didn't feel attached to her. My mind kept returning to how she was conceived, and I cried at all hours of the day. I asked God to deliver me from the pain in my heart. I used these Scripture verses to get me through: Joshua 1:9, "Have I not commanded you? Be strong and of good courage; do not be afraid, nor be dismayed, for the Lord your God is with you wherever you go." (NKJV). Psalm 27:14, "Wait on the Lord; Be of good courage, And

He shall strengthen your heart; Wait, I say, on the Lord!" (NKJV).

Working on base was a blessing. I could walk with my head held high. I had a place to stay, and most importantly, I earned a good paycheck. I saved some money and assisted with my daughter's expenses. Although I was still haunted by shame and guilt, I checked up on her and Miss Morgan every time I was given a day off. It felt good owning my life. It felt awesome not being obligated to anyone. Sometimes I cried due to loneliness, but I could move around freely. I felt like a strong woman.

While I was able to check on my child and Miss Morgan, I yearned for my birth mother. She was missing in my life. I longed to see her and my siblings. I had not seen them since my daughter turned one, two years ago. I wondered if they ever thought or asked about me. Did they even try to find me? Those worries crept into my thoughts and haunted me. I cried until I fell asleep, then decided to go and see her. I had nothing to lose. I was no longer scared of Ruggles. I could defend myself now.

On one of my days off, I decided to visit her. As I approached the gate to the house, I heard his voice right behind me. "What are you doing here?" I felt my body freeze, and fear consumed me. I didn't know what he was going to do. Memories flashed back in my mind of all the embarrassment he caused me and the frequent abuses I endured at his hands. I turned around quickly to face him. I answered, "I came to see my mom." He said, "I don't want you here." I used my favorite phrase, "As long as my mother lives here, I am coming to visit her. You cannot stop me. She is my mother." He stretched his hands out towards me. I didn't wait. I moved my body to the side and watched him almost fall before he caught the gate and steadied himself. It seemed like we were going to fight outside the gate. I was a young soldier. I depended on my training to stand up against this cruel man. He decided to use his body to block me from entering through the gate, but that didn't deter me. I told him I was still going inside to see my mother. I grabbed him by his hair, wrapped my other hand around his neck, and pulled him down.

My mother and siblings heard the commotion and ran to the gate. My mother begged me to let him go. I looked down at him and said, "If you ever put your hands on my mom again, you will have me to contend with." One of his locks came out. He picked it up, looked at me, turned to my mom, and said, "Your daughter pulled my hair out." I was a little worried about her because I knew what he would do to her after I left.

A Child Cries

I couldn't tell if she was happy to see me or not. We didn't get the chance to hug. I didn't even get the opportunity to speak with her because I could see the fear in her eyes as she begged me to leave. I couldn't tell her that I was doing well. The pain in my heart returned to full force. I started to hate this man all over again. Rage and bitterness consumed me, and all I wanted to do was kill him, but I walked away.

I hung around the parameters to listen for any commotion indicating that he was beating my mom after he thought I had left. I sat in the shaded corner of a cozy place called Chelsea's Jerk Center across the street, waiting to pounce on this aggressive villain called my stepfather. I knew I had to leave when night approached and head back to base. Nothing happened at the house that day.

I had already made up my mind that day to return. The weekend finally came, and I was free to leave the base again. I headed straight to my mom and discovered with relief that he wasn't there. I was happy to see my family again and could finally share my new experiences. I talked about my daughter and how she went to live in Portland with Miss Morgan. I talked about how Miss Morgan played an essential role in my decisions that led me to where I was. I was happy to catch up with my sisters too. They told me they all wanted to run away with me, but that was impossible then. We were all having such a good time together that we didn't notice how quickly the time had passed. Suddenly, I turned around just in time to see my stepfather coming toward me. I sprang up, looked at him, and noticed the broom flying towards me. I stood still and said to him, "If you hit me, I will kill you."

He came towards me and hit me with the broomstick. I held on and slapped him with it. He made the mistake of letting go of the broom. He said, "So, you are bad and want to fight me in my own house?" He was coming at me barehanded now. I picked up the broom with my foot, wheeled it as hard as I could, and hit him across the back. He fell, and I didn't see him move. I waited. He groaned but didn't get up as he lay there in pain. I then dropped the broom and walked away. That was when I knew he was only a weak man. I noted it. Before I left the house, I warned him that the next time he put his hands on my mom, I would chop them off. The next day, I found out that he was in the hospital. I had fractured his back. None of my siblings told me or mentioned the news. They just asked me to come by. I love to cook, so I made food for them that they couldn't cook.

We were happy together for the few days that he was away. I went there every chance I could after work and. I got to spend quality time with my siblings and my mom.

A Child Cries

My mom felt free; she could laugh and talk without looking over her head. My sisters weren't allowed to leave the house except for school, so we took the opportunity to walk through the town and see a movie at the then New Kingston Cinema, five minutes from the house. I brought them treats too. It was like Christmas for them. They finally got a taste of freedom as he was not around to control their whereabouts with his iron hand. They could hardly wait to see me arrive every evening. It was the most fun they had ever had; they had the time of their lives. When it was time for him to return home from the hospital, everyone was sad. My time of visiting every day at any time was over. We were about to hit the factory setting—back to fighting my stepfather to visit my mom.

A few weeks after he returned home, I got a call while at work. Ruggles was beating my mom. I asked to be excused from my duty and informed my staff sergeant that my mom was in trouble. When I arrived, he ran away. I asked my siblings what happened, and they told me he had a visitor, and the man asked about my mom. He wasn't pleased with the greeting, so he waited until the man had left and gave her a beating. I checked on my mom, and my heart shattered when I saw her face. I had tried to get her to leave on many occasions, but she refused. Hence, I know it was useless to ask again. It still pained me that she wouldn't go. At the time, she had three toddlers in the house. She had birthed seven children for him, and because of this, she thought she couldn't go to anyone or anywhere with seven children. I still don't know why she was so adamant not to leave a man who was battering her, but I stayed with her the entire day in case he returned. He knew that I would have to return to base before curfew, so I presumed that he showed up late at night. God knows I would have killed him if he had shown up, but God had a better plan for my life.

When I got back to base, I couldn't sleep. I didn't know what was happening at my mother's house, which made me anxious and terrified. It was painful leaving my mom and siblings at the behest of that monster. I decided to pray, "Lord Jesus, my needs are deeper than I know right now. Your gracious provisions for me on the cross go far beyond my needs. Lord, I am in mourning for my mother. Please, comfort her now, Jesus. She is thirsty and needs to be filled up with your presence. Heal the wounds and the pain that's been inflicted on her. In your name, I pray. Amen."

Chapter 6

Sadness

I was in the parish of St. Ann for a few months on training. I couldn't wait to see my mom and my siblings again. My mom and I had started bonding and building a relationship. I couldn't wait to talk to my siblings again to lift their spirits and bring them treats.

When I returned to my home base, I went to the house as soon as possible. Ruggles decided he didn't want me around anymore because he installed barbed wire and added a lock onto the gate. His pitiful effort to keep me out was futile because I climbed over the gate and was in the yard. I was even more determined to see my family after I had landed on the other side of the gate, but he was standing in front of me. It quickly turned into a shouting match, using our favorite words.

"Get out. Leave my house."

"I am not leaving until I see my mom. As long as she lives here, I will visit her."

The shouting intensified, and we started throwing punches at each other. We caused such an uproar that my siblings heard and came around to see.

By the time they arrived, I had wrapped his hair around a small fruit tree and poured kerosene oil on him, ready to set him ablaze. I was fed up with this abusive man who controlled my mom and siblings and made it difficult for me to communicate and have a thriving relationship with them. I held the matchbox in my hand and was ready to strike a match to set him on fire. As I opened the matchbox, a quiet gentleman came up and held me like a father. I recognized him as the gentleman who lived with his family on another part of the property. He calmly spoke to me, "Daughter, don't do it. I understand how you feel, but they will lock you up, so I won't allow you to do this." He took the matchbox from my hand, and I cried in his arms.

My stepfather ruined the moment and yelled at me to untie him. I wiped my face with my hands and turned to him. "How does it feel? You are in my control now." So many thoughts coursed through my head when I stared at him. I wanted to bring so much pain to him. He'd been

Sadness

beating my mom for years, and I wanted to know when it would finally stop. I turned around and left the house with everyone standing there. I went back to the base and cried my soul out in the privacy of my apartment. I asked God to kill him. I begged Him to listen to me. Why was He doing this to me?

When I calmed down, I remembered a song about God. I remembered that God's grace and mercy brought me through. He sent an angel to stop me from making a mistake that would ruin my life and keep me away from my family for a very long time. I was living this moment because of Him. I needed to thank and praise Him. I calmed to some degree, but I was still anxious. I wanted to call my family. Back then, we only had a home phone. If I called, I knew he would answer. I didn't know what had happened after I left, so I was scared for them. I couldn't sleep.

I knew I had to see my mom somehow, so I confided in my batch mate, Sheryl. She and I had become friends during our training and were now roommates. She and I devised a plan that night and carried it out the next day.

I got my mom to come to the back of the property, where there was an open lot. I carried goodies and groceries to my mom for her and my siblings. I also gave her some cash to buy whatever she wanted when he wasn't around. Before I left, my mom asked if I could not come around so that she could live her life in peace. My heart broke. I felt like a bus had run me over. I never understood the things that she had put up with from him. I told her, "I am your second child. I was still your child when he met both of us. Now, he wants to separate us for good." I could see the sadness in her eyes and the tears she was holding back. I didn't respond to her request. I stood there and let the words sink in. I developed even more hatred in my heart for that wicked man.

Chapter 7

Pain And More Pain

I tried to live and develop a new routine that didn't include visiting my family for my mom's sake. Staying away from them was hard, but I did it for her and my siblings' peace and safety. After a few months, I couldn't stay away any longer, so I decided to go and see her. I planned only to show myself if I knew he wasn't there.

When I approached the gate, I noticed that it was open. The place seemed empty. Had they gone out? I pushed the gate open and walked inside. My heart was skipping beats and hammering in my ears. When I walked inside, I was incredibly shocked! The house was empty.

I steadied myself and sat on the steps. I voiced a deep, loud cry to God. "Why are you doing this to me? Why?

A Child Cries

Why me?" My family was gone! My mom and siblings were nowhere to be found. There was no one around to give me any information or to say where they were. I was lost for words and distraught; I couldn't describe how I felt. I didn't have anyone to call, so I cried as the deluge of tears threatened to drown me. "Where could they have gone?" I didn't know what to do so I called the police.

I told them that I thought that man had killed my mom. They asked me what proof I had. I answered, "Nothing." They said, "All you are doing is wasting our time. Go and look for your family. When you find them, call us." They drove out of the compound and left me sitting on the steps with my knees weak and shaking; I couldn't move.

I called Sheryl. She thought something was wrong with me because I was crying uncontrollably. She asked me where I was and told me I was in New Kingston. She was surprised. "You went back to the house?" I told her I did and informed her that no one was there. She asked in a surprised tone, "What happened?" I sobbed and told her, "The house is empty. They are all gone."

The disappearance left a big hole in my heart. I moped around for days, unaware of my family's whereabouts. I still didn't know who to ask. I also didn't know his friends, so I couldn't ask them if they knew where he had moved. I was in extreme pain, but my pain is what made me strong.

Pain And More Pain

I kept on asking God to keep my mind safe from anxious thoughts. Sometimes, I felt like I was going crazy. I sat in the night and cried; that was my comfort. I knew that tears were a language that God understood, and He, alone, understood all I was going through.

A year passed, and I celebrated my twentieth birthday. I thought about my family and thanked God for another year. I was blessed to be in the land of the living. What a mighty God we serve. I decided to spend the weekend in Portland with my daughter and give her quality time and attention. I also decided to see my grandmother because I hadn't seen her in a while and was in the area.

I arrived at my grandma's house. She greeted me with a half-smile which I couldn't tell whether was genuine or not. I understood that she was getting older and more withdrawn and reserved. After we settled in and talked, the air got a little lighter. We had a great time talking and spending time together. I told her I didn't know where my mom and siblings were. Grandma always talked about my mom. She told me that she was a little disappointed in my mom's choices. My grandma had high hopes for her; I could hear the pain in her voice. She told me how she hated Ruggles. She said, "If I die, he should never come to my funeral because I will open my eyes on him." We shared a great laugh. Our time together was meaningful and well spent.

I had to head back to base since it was almost nighttime. I waved goodbye and got on the bus. As I was on the bus, I wondered, *Where are my mom and siblings?* I still didn't know where to start looking or what could have happened to them. I moved to the back of the bus, where no one could see the tears running down my face. My heart throbbed for them. I was dying to see my mom. I just wanted to make sure she was okay and not hurting. I prayed to God to shield her. I asked myself, *Where could he have taken her?* I turned to my faith and the Word of God to keep me going.

Chapter 8

I Have A Winning Faith

The experiences of each phase of your life were not made by the things that you see; they were made by the Word of God. I have learned to speak to my storms because my faith speaks to shape my future. My faith is my victory; I am a victor, not a failure; I am the head, not the tail; I am alive and not dead; my faith is tenacious; it cannot be defeated; it overcomes all things; I am going to win.

Despite his problems, a man who carried countless demons still desired to get to Jesus. He wanted to worship the Master and must have known that in Christ was His deliverance grounded. He chanted, "I am going to get to the Master. No matter the demon or the storm, I will drag it to Jesus and place it at his feet. I know He will help me overcome it."

A Child Cries

God has a great plan for every life. Sometimes, what people call misfortunes could be God's favor working in their lives. Sometimes, people may think you are a useless child, but God speaks in silence. I will pass through what I must pass through. God has prepared me for a more excellent and better place. My storm will make room for me.

My new change of mind was working for my betterment, but a high-ranking personnel officer was trying to change that. He was determined to make my life a living hell. I was scheduled for morning training, so I had to wake up earlier than my fellow officers. I had to put in extra work. I would be scolded for anything and eventually had to go to lock up for disobeying orders, which was fine. I didn't realize that this was all a ploy so that he could get personal and familiar with me. I rejected his advancements and refused to entertain him. As a result, my life became more and more complicated.

He decided that I would work in a different facility off-base. I had to work in the 'Naffei,' which meant I had no more free time. I was always scheduled to work more hours than the other officers. I also had to learn how to drive a truck to get there. I was afraid, but God made a promise to me that He would not leave me. I passed the driving test and could drive to work, but I didn't drive back to the barracks after work. Sheryl would come and wait for me to finish work so we could walk back together. She knew I was afraid to leave work and drive back to the barracks alone because that high-ranking personnel officer was still trying to get me to sleep with him.

All my friends were taking different courses and being promoted to higher ranks, while I remained a private. I told myself I would not become another victim of an unfortunate circumstance. I was determined to make the most of my career, but I didn't have to try too hard or compromise my values. I fell in love with the change and the new location. It was good, and I was free. Working in the Naffei wasn't a punishment; I was happy. I didn't know where my mom was, so all I wanted to do was bury myself in work to save more. I wanted to take my mom and siblings away from that man. I finally could afford a place of my own, so I started living off base.

I began attending Saint Luke's Anglican church, which is in Cross Road, and got involved in the activities there. The church did an excellent job in molding and shaping me. It helped me to let go of my anger. I didn't trust or believe in anyone, but I got close to Sister Margaret, to who I entrusted and related my feelings. She insisted that I release all my anger and bitterness. Her heart was loving and kind. I even became friends with the pastor's mother of the church. She invited me to the deaconesses' house, where we had prayer circles. She encouraged me to do good and allow myself to be guided in the right direction by God. I ended up living at the deaconesses' house for a while which gave me peace of mind. I stayed there until I could live in the church's apartments. Those apartments were only for church members and cute, upscale apartments. I was smiling when I moved in. My life was gradually becoming that of a grown-up woman living independently.

I started to make new friends at the church. One of my friends was Tracia Brown, whose dad was a DJ. On some of my off workdays, I would go out and hang with Tracia and my other friends. Sometimes Tracia and her dad would throw a party at their house, and I would go if I could. After attending parties a few times, I became great friends with Tracia and everyone else.

One night, I met a guy at one of the parties. He was a nice guy named Alvin. For several months, we went out for dinner and a few movies. He kept up his gentlemanly behavior the entire time and wasn't creepy. He had good manners, too; He was almost too good to be true. One weekend, we decided to go to a live show where the group, Manhattan, was performing. We bought tickets and attended the show. The show finished in the early morning, about 5 am. On our way home, he asked if he could stop by his house, which was off Hagley Park Road. It wasn't a bad area, so we stopped at his home so he could pick up whatever he claimed he needed to retrieve.

After about ten minutes, an older, pleasant gentleman, Mr. Stewart, greeted me. "Good morning, young lady. I don't think it's a very good idea for you to stay in the car." He also informed me that Alvin was in the bathroom. I trusted him as he had a fatherly mannerism. I walked into the house with him, and after talking for some time, I fell asleep. It had been more than sixteen hours since I last slept, and I was fighting the exhaustion. I dozed off, and the next thing I knew, Alvin was kissing me. I rejected it and told him that I needed to go home and that he should let me leave. He started saying that we'd been seeing each other for months, and it was time to take it to the next level. My heart was beating so hard! I told him that I wasn't ready and that we should wait. But he was standing in front of me, asking me what I thought he should do about his thing that was standing at attention. I looked at him puzzled and replied, "I don't know." He came after me, and I dashed off. One thing led to another, and I didn't go back to see him.

All my memories came back. I didn't talk about it with anyone. I tried to return to my everyday life as though nothing had happened. He called a few times, but I never answered.

A Child Cries

It was months after that incident. I didn't have any illness or anything; just living and enjoying my life as best as possible. I had blocked out everything that had happened to me. One day while I was sitting at my desk, I felt a sharp pain in my back, like someone had smacked me hard. I made a bellowing cry that captured the attention of everyone in the office. It was eight months before I went to the doctor. He said I was okay. I left the doctor feeling okay until my coworker took me to the sick bay on the base. After going through some tests, the doctor called a few days later and asked me to come in. When I arrived at the sick bay, I discovered I was pregnant. I told him that it couldn't be possible. He assured me that I was fully eight months pregnant. I didn't know what to say or how to respond.

I left the base and went home to do what I knew how to do best—cry! How is it that I wasn't showing any signs or feeling different like my last pregnancy? I didn't gain any weight, and nothing was different in my life. I went to Saint Andrew's hospital. I needed to know what was going on with me. After some tests, I found out that the baby wasn't in my womb but was outside of the womb. Now, my life turned upside down again. I asked myself, "What do I do? How do I tell this man I am pregnant when I haven't spoken to him in months?" That wasn't my biggest worry, though the Army was. I had to tell my Major what happened. I was doing so well, and now this storm came to blow me away. I asked God, "What did I do to deserve this? God, please, work this out for me."

I got the courage to go to Alvin's job and tell him I was eight months pregnant. He looked at me like something was wrong. He responded, "What do you want me to do?" We spoke a little more, and then I left.

After a few weeks, I felt like something had hit me in the back again, but with more gruesome pain. I gasped in agony, but no one knew what was happening to me. I noticed a growing bulge on my left side which shocked everyone. I was rushed to the hospital. The doctor came over to me and said, "We'll have to take you to the Kingston Public Hospital." From the expressions on the faces around me, I knew that something was wrong. The pain was terrible. My mind flashed black to my mother. I needed my mom, but I still didn't know where she was. I didn't understand why I was in such excruciating pain. Was I dying? What was happening? Was I going into labor? I wasn't prepared for any of this. Even after discovering I was pregnant, I hadn't had the chance to buy things for the baby. I asked the nurse to call my aunt Merl. She said she couldn't come, but thank God my two cousins, Linette and Marie, came. After they arrived, the nurse informed me that the baby had breached the womb and was in a dangerous place that could take my life.

A Child Cries

I wished my mother was there with me. I cried out for my mom as tears flooded my face. I shouted, "I'm going to die!" The doctors came over to me; one of them was an African doctor. He assured me he would do everything he could to save my life. I remembered that there was a nurse there who was also pregnant. Her name was Martin. She took my hand, placed it on her belly, and said, "I am having twin babies. What do you think I should name them?" I realized she was trying to distract me from thinking about my situation.

With tears streaming down my face, I replied, "I don't know." She nodded and kept on rubbing my stomach. She asked, "Can I pray with you?" I nodded because no words would come from my mouth. The nurse prayed for a safe delivery and told me that she would come to check on me from time to time. I thanked her then, contacted the child's father, and let him know that I was in the hospital with complications. He said, "I won't come to the hospital because I'll pass out." That felt like a knife thrust through my heart. I could now see that I had no one. I felt utterly alone in the world without the support from my mom, siblings, or even the father of my child. That old pain came charging like a crazy bull.

I was in labor for six hours, usually trying to have the baby. After many attempts, the doctor informed me that the baby wasn't turning. He said that he would try to turn the baby. After the first try, I had an emergency and started bleeding. The nurses ran to help me.

One nurse came to me and asked, "Do you have anyone who would take the baby?

I asked her, "What do you mean?" Am I dying?

She looked at me and said, "Your case is different."

I asked her, "What does that mean?"

She said, "Your child is in your back, and his feet are turned downward. We must do an operation right now, but we need someone to sign these papers."

"I want my mother!" I cried aloud. I didn't know where she was, so the nurse asked me who I could call. I said, "My aunt." After a few hours in indescribable pain, she finally showed up. She was reluctant to sign the papers but finally agreed and signed them. She came to tell me before the operation that someone had told her where my mother was. She said she sent my mom a message but was still waiting on her to respond. After that, she left.

From that moment, I wasn't aware of anything else that happened. I felt like I was in a dream. I could hear people talking, but I couldn't respond. I could tell who came, but I couldn't see anyone. After I woke up, I found

A Child Cries

out that I had been in a coma since the operation in September. I saw my cousins that same day, and after a bit of chit-chat with them, I found out that my baby was still in the hospital. They told me that he weighed thirteen pounds and fourteen ounces, only two ounces away from being fourteen pounds! He was a big baby. They laughed, but I couldn't. I could only think *that my baby was still in the hospital for all those months, and no one cared to take him in until I woke up*. The pain in my heart was more than I could bear. I wanted to see my baby, and later that day, the nurse brought me to see him. All he did was look at me and smile. I didn't want them to take me back without him; I wanted him to stay in my bed, but I went back alone.

I tried to find out if they found my mom or anyone who knew where she lived. I could have passed away, and my mom wouldn't have known. *My stepfather is a wicked man!* I kept thinking.

I spent three and a half months in the hospital without a single visit from the father or his family. I later learned that he didn't want me to have a son but a daughter. After leaving the hospital, he visited to see if my son looked like him. He then started to visit every two weeks and would contribute one hundred Jamaican dollars to the baby's upkeep and then ask how his son was doing. His visits and the money meant nothing to me. He wasn't performing the role of a birth father, and my son needed a special kind of formula with iron, which cost more than the hundred dollars he contributed. I was determined to help my child and do my best to keep my life on track.

Chapter 9

Finding Mom

One day, I was on my way going about my business when I heard someone calling my name. I looked around to see a gentleman approaching me. He asked, "Are you Ruggles's stepdaughter?" I nodded. He said, "I have been looking for you for three years. Your mom asked me to tell you where she and your siblings lived. I was the one who helped them move. They live in the parish of Saint Mary in a place called Oracabessa." Oh, that was such good news to me! My mom missed big things in my life, like my second pregnancy and the birth of my baby boy. He continued, "I can tell you how to get there." He then gave me the address and the directions on how to reach their new place.

A Child Cries

I immediately called my family to give them the news and devised a plan to get there. I asked my friend to accompany me to see my mom and siblings because I knew I would get into an argument with Ruggles.

Before my mission to find my mother, I had to see my grandmother. It had been about a month since I got the information, and I wanted to update my grandmother about this new development personally. I took her monthly groceries to her house, gave her the news, and then talked. Unlike before, we now had a cordial relationship, especially since I was the only grandchild that visited her. There wasn't any sign of her "special" grandchild, and my grandma stopped asking about her. After the chat, I left and headed back to work.

The long-awaited day was here. My journey to go and see her and my siblings were in view. I brought along my friend, Noel, and my son. We arrived at the location and followed the directions given to us. Going up the hill towards the house, I met a lady with dreadlocks. I greeted her and asked if she knew about the people that moved here about three years ago.

She said, "Yes, I know the dread, his wife, and his children."

I smiled and said, "That lady is my mom, and I am trying to find her and my siblings."

She said, "My name is Ragga."

I told her, "Nice meeting you. Do you think you could take me to their house?"

She said, "Yes, man."

We exchanged a few more pleasantries, had a few laughs, and talked about my baby. I told her I surprised my mom with my baby.

We arrived at the house, and I handed my son to Noel. Ragga called out, "Dread, I have some visitors for you."

When he came out and saw me, the smile on his face faded away. He said to me, "What are you doing here? How did you find my house?" I stood there looking at him.

I said, "I am here to see my mom."

He replied, "Leave my house."

I replied, "I am not going anywhere until I see my mom."

Ragga stepped in, "Dread, she is here already and traveled so far to see her mom and to surprise her with her new grandson. Let her see her mom.

He replied, "I left Kingston to be at peace away from her."

"Am I a bother to you?" I asked.

He didn't reply. He just said, "I want you to leave my house."

I shouted out for my mom. "Mama, mama!"

My sister, Aldine, appeared at the door. She was followed by my sisters, Ava and Toby. Then came my brother, Wade, followed by my younger brothers. My mother was the last one to go to the door. She didn't know what was happening but heard my siblings' commotion. She stood in the doorway just looking like she had seen a ghost, and then a smile appeared on her face.

I started to walk toward her. Noel stood and watched me as I walked toward my mom. My stepfather didn't try to approach me mainly because Ragga was talking to him. I couldn't hear what she was saying to him because my heart was beating so loudly. I was only focused on seeing my mom and siblings. When I reached her, I asked why she had left without telling me. She said that Ruggles only told her that they were moving the day before, and she couldn't reach me. "It all happened so fast. I asked the truck driver to find you and tell you where we were." I nodded. I was so happy to see my mom and know she was okay. I was also still trying to understand why he hated me so much that he wanted me out of my mother's and siblings' lives. There was a wedge between us that he planted from the beginning.

I didn't leave that night. Ragga offered us accommodation so I could spend another day with my family. I was sad when it was time to go, and I could also see the sadness on my sisters' and brothers' faces. I promised to come and see them as often as I could.

Now that I found them again, I started to visit them more often. I thought things were getting better for us, but one day, I visited, and he said, "I don't want you to come back." He continued, "You are putting bad things into my children's minds. You are corrupting their minds."

My day went from sunshine to darkness. I felt like a knife was thrust into my heart. I left and went home. I was up the night thinking about my childhood. Back then, I was the loner in the family. I asked God to help me, please. I felt like I had no hope. My life was snatched from me, and I was going down the same path I feared. How could this keep happening to me? Those thoughts led me to decide that I had to make a change for the better. I had to live my life. God, help me live! I didn't know how it felt to be loved. I desperately wanted to be loved and not feel abandoned. How could I make it? "God, can't you see me? God, where are you? This is an emergency. I never gave up running toward God.

I didn't go back to visit my mom and my siblings for a few months. I was tired of this man insulting me. I just wanted my family and the opportunity to live like other people and their families in happiness.

I had been battered and abused by men all my life. My father abandoned me; my uncle molested me; my stepfather left me to suffer; my daughter's father raped me, and my son's father violated me and left me with the lion's share of the responsibility to take care of our son. I was feeling displaced, lonely, and abandoned by my family. All these people left me with scars. The system had battered me, and now I was only trying to survive. I gave up on my dreams when I got pregnant in the middle of high school. I was now a mother, so I had to hustle to feed my children. I didn't get any support from their fathers because I decided I was no one's baby mama. However, throughout all this, God stood by my side.

After Ruggles told me not to come back, I went to my grandmother's house since we now had a good relationship. I gave her the latest updates about my mom and told her that I wasn't going back to his house anytime soon. "Ruggles doesn't want me there, so I am not going back. I will leave them in peace because, according to Ruggles, I am disrupting their home life with my frequent visits. It is best if I don't go back."

It had been a year, and I still hadn't gone back to visit my mom and siblings. One of my stepfather's close friends informed me that they were coming back to live in Kingston. Mr. Mortimer Planner, or "the Professor," as I liked to call him because he taught at the University of West Indies, was a good man. I first met him when he visited our home. He was a good friend of Ruggles. I had a friend who attended the university who ran into him. He asked about me, and she gave him my information. We spoke for a while on the phone, and he informed me that he knew how badly his friend had treated me. He told me that he would help me out. He said that Ruggles was considering returning to Kingston. He promised to send me more information when he had all the details.

I'd been waiting to hear from him, and each day became more and more uncertain. While waiting for the professor, my son and I moved and now live in Franklin Town. It was hard going to base and finding a place for him to stay while I went to work. I had no family members to assist me, but I found a way to manage my daily routine. It was several months after the move when he called. We briefly chatted, and he told me they were moving in a week. He didn't know the location yet. He called back after some days to tell me they would be arriving in Kingston in two days near Browns Town in East Kingston. I didn't know where that was, but I was resolved to find out where it was. The professor called again to give me the correct address and directions to get to the house. He also warned me not to go there immediately. "Give him some time to settle in. He will want to find out where you got the new address."

I planned to go with my cousin, Marie. The day finally arrived, and we approached the gate of the new residence at the address I was given. I knocked on the gate, and Ruggles appeared. When he opened the gate and saw my face, his expression changed.

"Good afternoon," I said.

He didn't respond with the same pleasantries. "What are you doing here?"

His response was nothing new to me. He was adamant that I wasn't supposed to have any communication with my mom and siblings. I didn't respond to him; instead, I started shouting so my mom or siblings would hear me and come outside. When I looked at the house, I saw my sister Nancy at the door. She turned her head and shouted, "Mama, Jackie is at the gate!" Soon, all my other siblings came out to look at me. They all had big grins on their faces. Then my mom came out. I could see that she was holding back her smile. She couldn't show it because if Ruggles saw it, it would be a war between them.

My cousin, Marie, walked past him and Miss Joe. Miss Joe was what all my mom's nieces called her. Actually, everyone called her that. I went in behind her and started hugging all of them. I was so happy to see them again. My heart sometimes hurt at the thought that I wasn't as close to them because of their dad, but I tried not to focus on that when I saw them. Ruggles didn't say anything to me for the rest of that day. He just walked away from the house, allowing us the space and privilege to bond. I know he was upset and curious about how I found out the address of where they lived since they had just moved there. But I didn't dwell on that man. I enjoyed my time with my family. After spending the day there and catching up, it was time for me to leave.

My cousin and I talked about the day's outcome when I broke down in tears. I couldn't wrap my head around it. Why? Why did this man hate me so much? What did I do to him? He met my mom with her two daughters and then proceeded to do everything he could to separate us from her. He succeeded with Michelle, who our grandma took in. She later moved in with our aunt Merlene and kept her distance.

A Child Cries

On the other hand, I refused to stay away; my mother and siblings meant too much to me. I remember Marie trying to comfort me. "Jacks, all is going to be well soon." When I thought back on my childhood traumas, rape, rejection, and molestation, it made me develop more anger toward that dreadful man. He was responsible for everything that happened to me. He made me suffer and affected the lens through which I experienced my life. As I cried my millionth tear, I was vexed in my spirit. I pulled myself together long enough to thank my cousin for coming with me, then bid her goodbye.

When I returned home, I curled up in my bed and was plagued by negative thoughts. I asked myself about my dad, mom, grandma, and stepfather. I wondered, *what had I done to deserve such unkindness from the ones I loved?* I gave my all to everyone who had come across my path. I compromised and sacrificed my personal feelings for them. Despite what I was going through, I still showed love and compassion to everyone. Why couldn't I get the same in return? My heart yearned to be loved by my mom. I felt alone. I imagined what I wanted to do and what I wanted to become in my life. I thought about how my mom could not help my dreams come through because she made a bad decision to live with the wrong man.

Tears were my language, and I knew God was the only one who understood them. I didn't share my inner thoughts with anyone because I didn't have anyone to talk to. No one knew the whole story of my life or the full extent of the pain I was suffering. I was a smart street girl and lived like that for many years because I was forced to. I had to adapt because I had been tossed and kicked out so many times by my stepfather. I had to know how to maneuver my life when I was living from place to place with any family who took me in. I didn't want to go through another trauma in my life. I told myself, "I will be safe no matter what." I didn't trust anyone anymore.

I had a good friend who stood by my side during those dark days. He would do anything for my safety. He guarded me with his life and made sure nothing happened to me. That friend was Noel. God sent him into my life at just the right time. When I thought I was going crazy or the road seemed rocky, and the emptiness had set in, he was there. The days didn't look so dark with him by my side. Noel was my strength and my shoulder to cry on. He was my best friend. He encouraged me when it seemed like I couldn't make it. His smile improved things, and his hugs seemed to bring out the sun on my bad days. His caring words significantly changed me and kept me thinking of better days. He was the watchman over my life. I was afraid

A Child Cries

to love or trust men, and Noel understood that I needed to heal from them.

It was time for another visit to my mom's new residence. I arrived there and found my mom badly beaten by Ruggles. My sisters were crying, and my mom kept telling me, "Please leave this house." She told me that she would deal with him, but clearly, she couldn't deal with this wicked and weak man who only had the strength to beat women. I got mad and asked about his whereabouts. Again, I asked her to leave, but she refused. I was going to kill him. I went out trying to find him, but he was nowhere to be found. I called a few of my friends to come over and assist me in finding him but to no avail. I stayed there for the whole day, but he stayed away from the house. Early in the morning, I left but not before I asked my mom again to come with me. She refused again. I couldn't force her to go, so I hugged her goodbye.

I left with my heart feeling heavy. I could do nothing, and that thought left me feeling hopeless and upset. I had to control my feelings, though. I decided to focus on how I could kill him. I had planned his death in my mind for years to get back at him for all the things he had done to my mother and me. The pain in my heart was too much after seeing my mom. When I got home, I called Noel, and he immediately came over. As usual, he counseled me into not putting my plan into action and making any wrong decisions. "While it is tempting, killing him would only hinder you from reaching your destiny. God will take care of everything and everyone in due time and season. Everything depends on how you choose to live. Please remember, you have two beautiful children looking up to you."

After he left, I stayed home and sobbed until I fell asleep. I woke up to a brand-new day with high hopes and possibilities for better days. I told myself, "If it's the last thing I do, I will do it well. I will get my mom to leave that man. I am going to work hard to take her away from his control, somewhere she can find happiness and peace of mind. I will choose life and keep living it; I am going to live and not die." I chose to live with gratitude for my love for my kids, the love that filled my heart, the peace that rests within my spirit, and the voice of hope that says, "All things are possible."

Chapter 10

Sisterly Love

My two youngest sisters were all grown up, and ready to leave the nest. Every time I went to visit, they constantly told me that they wanted to come and live with me. I didn't know what to say to them. Their father thought that I was a bad influence on them and needed to leave him and all his children alone. He wanted me gone because I was a big threat to him. He knew I was not afraid of him, and that I would not back down from him. He knew I would stand up to him and fight him like a man. The last time I was there, I told him again, "If you ever put your hands on my mom again, those hands will be mine." I wasn't joking anymore. I even planned with some of my squad members to drive there the next time he whipped her again. He wasn't responsible for me hadn't been for years. He knew I was owning the world and doing well. I bet he didn't expect me to turn out that way. He had said some negative stuff about my life when I visited once, but sometimes I wonder if he saw greatness in me.

My sisters were constantly beseeching, so we came up with a plan of how and when to make the move with them. They didn't have a life if they continued living with him. They lacked exposure to the world and existed in a cocoon of control. They weren't taught how to defend themselves or how to talk to people. They were shy with no social skills. They were even afraid to approach the gate by themselves! We made the plan in secret because we knew that if their father found out about it then he would beat them. My sisters and I bonded quite well for the first time in our lives over this plan. I had to put a plan in place on my end too, and study how and when to execute it. Currently, my place was only for my son and I, so I now had to find a place that could accommodate all of us. I had to make room for them it was my sisterly sacrifice of love.

My third youngest sister wasn't in our plans. She had passed her exams to get into high school. She would be moving and living with her grandparents so that she could be closer to the school. I was happy for her because she would be exposed to a new and better way of life. My youngest sister, Nancy, would be the only girl that remained in the house, and my three brothers would be there with her since they were the youngest of all.

I continued to visit my mom and siblings like normal, and everything was okay for a while. My stepfather and I didn't argue as much. He came to the understanding that he couldn't get rid of me, and so he tolerated me in the best way he could. He would leave the house on the days I visited and would only return when he thought I was gone. After some months, I found out that they were moving again into a house that he bought on King Street, which was a better place than East Kingston. That was good news for me because I knew about the move this time.

Still, I asked my mom, "I heard that you were moving again, weren't you going to tell me where?"

She said, "Watson didn't tell me anything about the move." Watson was his real name. I only nodded in response. My mom was the type of person to keep everything locked inside. She never shared with me any of her feelings on the abuse she went through. As far as I know, she never said anything to anyone.

It was time again for me to visit my grandma since I hadn't done so in a while. I had a lot of catching up to do. By then, she had gotten a little older and weaker and couldn't move about as well as she did before, so I had to go out more often when I visited her to do her daily activities in town. I knew that her breakfast had to be ready at 7am before we started our family chats. We would talk about what was going on in our lives, what had happened in and around the family circle, and more. We had a great time together chatting and bonding. My sister still couldn't find the time to visit her, and that would always be the next conversation topic. "Where is Jasmine?" I would lie, "Oh, work is taking up her time and then she gets off late." I would then try to switch the conversation to another topic.

My grandma would also give me the regular talk about the bills she had to pay down at Buff Bay, and I would tell her not to worry about them. I would tell her to just give me the bills, and I will pay them. I will do all that I have to do for you before I head back to Kingston. We also had a few heart-to-heart chats. She shared some stories of her travels, and of meeting people. I bid her farewell and told her that I would see her on my next visit. She was hard to please but could be fun to talk to if she was up to the task.

Grandma used to be a social butterfly, and a high-class woman. She always dressed fashionably back in the day because she was a seamstress. She told me she worked at a factory called, "Shamrock," in Kingston before she retired and moved back to Portland where she was born. She was also a part of the Ladies' Department at her church for many, many years. She was involved in a lot of the church departments. She still loved to sing even in her older years. Her favorite radio station was RJR. The gospel music would ring out at 6am, and everyone would have to be up and ready for singing. Her favorite Bible Scripture was Psalm 91 (NKJV). Her morning devotion was a must. She was also a teacher of life skills. That was very important to her. I learned how to cook from her since cooking was her specialty. She taught me how to wash and reminded me that, "The white has to be whiter." I learned many things from her. I think that was her way of loving because showing love was something she was afraid of doing. She may have been hurt in her past. Sometimes, I asked her about my grandfather, but she would never answer and spoke about him. I only knew that he was from another district in Portland because I have met some of his side of the family. My grandmother was a giver in her own right and people in Portland respected her.

Throughout the years, I supported my grandma in many ways. I wanted her to love me in the same way I loved and treated her, but she only had love for my sister. In my heart, I was hurt knowing that I was there for her, but her attention was only on my sister. Grandma was into me if I could provide information about my older sister.

Nevertheless, I had to learn to look beyond my feelings, so that I could do the best I could for her.

I felt like Hannah from the Bible. The name Hannah means "favor or grace." In the Bible, she was constantly provoked and misunderstood. When I read about her, my understanding was that her name meant that she would need both, favor, and grace, to overcome the relentless attacks from her adversaries. After understanding that, I asked God to provide me both favor and grace, so that I could continue to carry out my good work and my fierce love. I also thanked God for the type of heart he gave me. After paying her bills, cleaning the house, and washing her clothes, I headed back home to Kingston. I wished her all the love until I saw her again in two weeks. About a week and a half after my visit.

I was on my way to work. I received a call from a gentleman saying that my grandmother wanted me to come and visit her because all her bills needed to be paid. I was shocked because I had just visited her two weeks ago to check on her, and pay all her bills, and do all that she needed me to do. It was my birthday that week, so I informed the gentleman to tell her that I would come on the weekend to see her.

Saturday was my birthday, so I decided to spend it with my granny. I informed everyone in the family that I was going to visit her Saturday, so if they had anything to give her, I would take it to her. No one responded, so I picked up a few items for her and headed to Portland. Little did I know that, There was going to be a little surprise for me at Granny's that I knew nothing about.

After we had supper that Friday night, grandma related all the things I needed to know if she should "go home to be with the Lord." She gave me a stack of important papers then gave me all the details about other important documents such as land deeds. She gave me specific instructions and told me what belonged to who, and more. I noticed that my name wasn't mentioned in any land that she was giving away. At that time, I remembered thinking, *So, what about me? I have been by your side all this time and doing everything I do everything i could for you, but nothing for me?* I dismissed the thought, and instead, kept on listening to all her requests. I didn't know at the time that this was her saying goodbye to me and all of her family in her own way. I remembered her saying, "I need you to read me Psalm91 and whatever happens, God will bless you. I may not have been a good grandmother to you, but you have been a good granddaughter to me." I couldn't hold back my tears. That was the first time I ever felt any love from her. We then sang a few old songs and hymns. We laughed and talked until the wee hours of the morning.

A Child Cries

For the first time ever, she said, "Don't wake me up early, and turn off the radio." I was surprised. My grandmother's radio never went off. It stayed on the RJR station all day long because early in the morning the gospel songs would come on. I nodded, and we went to sleep.

I woke up to the sun's rays beaming through the window of the room that I had slept in for so many times in my life. I opened the window and picked a grapefruit from the tree outside my window. Once it was 6am, it was time for me to leave my room and start making breakfast. The radio wasn't turned off because of her request. Once I was done, I walked into the living room calling out, "Grandma! Grandma!" No response came back. I noticed that nothing had been open, not the windows of her room or her curtains. The living room was still dark and her room door was still closed. I walked up to her door and called her again, but still I received no answer. I pushed the door open and was greeted with my grandma looking like she was just sleeping. I touched her toes, and they felt cold. I quickly moved around to the top of her bed. I touched her face, and it was cold too. At that moment, I knew she had gone home to be with the Lord. I immediately got strength. I got dressed and went up the road to our family's house to inform them of the death of my grandmother.

I needed to take her body to the hospital in Buff Bay, so I waited for my cousin to come and assist me with her body. In the meantime, I dressed her and wrapped her up in a large comforter. When he arrived, we called someone with an open back truck to take her body to Buff Bay Hospital. The house had a twin bed in the back room. I asked my cousin and the driver to place the mattress in the back of the truck and I wrapped my grandmother's body and placed her on the mattress. I sat with her remains in the truck all the way to the hospital.

It was perplexing. I didn't cry at all because I made the determination to be strong for her, and everyone else. After the doctor pronounced her dead, I went to the Buff Bay Police Station and asked them to contact my family in Kingston. I became this super strong person, as though she had given me the strength and courage to carry out the task she had given me. I still haven't cried to this day. I spent the night at her house putting things into perspective and waiting for the other family members to arrive. I was feeling a great pain in my heart because she was no longer there for me to talk to. I stayed in her bed and wrapped myself up in her blanket.

While I talked aloud, I could hear her saying to me, "Pray."

A Child Cries

"I cannot!" I went back to the Psalm she had told me to read her the night before and it comforted me in that moment. I kept on asking God, "Is this a mistake? Is this a mistake? Why is it that everyone I love either hates me or doesn't love me at all? What have I done to deserve all of this unfair treatment?" I kept asking, but no answers came. I curled up, and eventually drifted off to sleep.

I was up bright and early preparing myself for everyone's arrival. I was still alone putting everything together, while convincing myself that I Could do it. I started making arrangements for food. Friends and family, in and around the district, started waiting for their arrival. My uncle was the first person to arrive, and all my memories of him and what he did to me just welled up inside of me. I didn't want him to ask or say anything to me because I was still feeling the hurt from what he had done to me as a child. I still hadn't told anyone about his abuse. I still didn't understand back then the real damage that he had done to my life, but I knew that the pain was real. I despise him and didn't want him near me. My heart hurts knowing he was my uncle.

The family that lived nearby arrived, and I felt more comfortable in their presence. My aunts and my mom and cousins were on their way and my sisters made their entrance. I was still trying to be strong for everyone. I was the one keeping everyone from breaking down. No one asked me how I was doing or if I was okay; I felt like nobody asked how> I'm doing. They didn't have empathy for me. Once everyone arrived, we all went down to the funeral morgue in Buff Bay to make arrangements. It was hard going to see my grandmother in the morgue knowing that I was the last one to see and talk with her. I remember her telling me that I was strong and would overcome any hardship that I faced. I could do this.

My aunt Merl took over the preparations for the program service of thanksgiving for my grandmother'. To my surprise, my aunt never mentioned my name or involved me in my grandmother's service and it broke my heart. I felt like I didn't exist in any form or frame among my family let alone strangers. Although I had been the one to do everything for her mother, she didn't even bother to include or acknowledge me. Instead, my aunt included my sister in the program arrangements and even gave her the opportunity to participate during the service. After that, I became cold towards my aunt Merl. Jasmine didn't even show up until the day before the funeral. She cried like she had been beside my grandmother all these years and actually missed her.

The day of the funeral my uncle and I got into a fight. When we got to the morgue to dress my grandma, I noticed that one of her teeth was missing. She wore a crown on her front tooth, but it was missing. After asking the staff, I was directed to the lady preparing her body. She informed me that my uncle had taken it. I went looking for him and questioned him then asked him to return it, but he refused. My hostility and displeasure towards him reached its peak after I found out that he took my grandma's tooth out on her funeral day. The rage that I held inside for him for years found a way out. I remembered what he did to me and how he had stolen my trust and youth. I became angrier and angrier. I came at him with a vengeance in my heart. I really smacked him hard and we started fighting. In the end, he decided to return the tooth. We went back to the morgue to place the crown back in her mouth, so we could finish the arrangements but the tooth didn't fit properly, so the lady fixed my grandma's face upwards so that no one would know.

At the church service, my heart was in pain because no one acknowledged me. I wasn't on the program and I wasn't asked to do anything, not even recount stories about the woman I had cared for, loved, and lived with for years. It shook my core but who could I talk to about it? No one! I couldn't even cry because I had to be strong. That pain made me stronger.

Sisterly Love

During the repast, everyone was enjoying themselves and having a good time. While they were carefree, I was hurting deep in my heart. What had I done to deserve such awful treatment from all the people who I cared for and loved? Was it really all because of my complexion, my abuse, or my determination to make my life better? I knew that my process wasn't going to be easy, but why? I have had to fight all my life to be the best because the people in my life weren't there to help me. I decided to put my feelings behind me. I put on a smile and a brave face and prepared my mind for the reading of the will. I didn't know at the time, but the real pain came when it was time to read the will. When the storms of life are raging over me, I have to keep moving forward. I handed the will to my aunt Merlene, who read the will aloud and not once was my name mentioned. I wanted to cry, but I didn't know how to. My sister, Michelle, was mentioned. She never once came to visit our grandma or bring her a meal. I did that. I was the one who went grocery shopping for her, visited and ensured that she was okay, and paid her bills. I did everything.

When it was all over, I went back home, and everything hit me like a runaway train. I cried and asked myself numerous questions. I prayed for the pain to go away. I told myself that I was special, and that God would make a way for me. I told God what I was going to become, all the places I would go, how I would travel the world, and that I didn't need anyone to validate me. I then read the Bible to comfort me. It was my storybook, and I soon drifted off to sleep.

Chapter 11

Words That Comforted Me

The Lord God Almighty said:

- I am unique: Psalm 139:14, "I will praise You, for I am fearfully and wonderfully made…"

- I am lovely: Daniel 12:3, "Those who are wise shall shine Like the brightness of the firmament, and those who turn many to righteousness Like the stars forever and ever."

- I am precious: 1 Corinthians 6:19, "Or do you not know that your body is the temple of the Holy Spirit who is in you, whom you have from God, and you are not your own?"

- I am strong: Psalm 18:32, "It is God who arms me with strength, and makes my way perfect."

- I am chosen: John 15:16, "You did not choose Me, but I chose you and appointed you that you should go and bear fruit, and that your fruit should remain, that whatever you ask the Father in My name He may give you."

The hymn, *'My hope is built on nothing less'* is one of my favorites and it comforted me in many dark hours:

"My hope is built on nothing less Than Jesus Christ, my righteousness;

I dare not trust the sweetest frame, but wholly lean on Jesus' name.

On Christ, the solid Rock, I stand; All other ground is sinking sand,

All other ground is sinking sand.

Jesus paid it all:

SIN… PAID SHAME… PAID

REGRETS…. PAID PAST MISTAKES… PAID UNFORGIVENESS… PAID HURTS… PAID ANGER…. PAID DEBT… PAID

Back at home, I continued with my day-to-day lifestyle, and tried to put all that had happened behind me. I didn't think I could do anything to make my relationship with my family members any better, so I decided to carry on with my life. From time to time, I'd find myself crying but it didn't change anything.

I still took care of my son and dealt with his father. He still visited and dropped money off. He still didn't spend any time with his son, but that was okay. I still visited my daughter in Port Antonio. Her dad didn't support her because I didn't want to become his, or any man's baby mama. I met a friend, who later became a best friend and sister to me close to where my daughter was living in Portland. I stayed with her whenever I visited my daughter. Her family became my family, and we always had a good time when I saw them. Her mom holds a special place in my heart because she encouraged me to make the best of what I had in the present time and create a plan. I was determined to work and put my money away for the better days ahead. I kept on telling myself, "My better days are ahead." I told myself, "I don't need a man to validate me in any form of my living." And that, "No one will stop me from getting to where I'm going. I can do this with help from the Lord."

A Child Cries

My life was simple, and I was truthful to myself. I accepted that I was going to be single and alone. I had tried to date men but found that they were never truthful to me and that turned me off from them. I didn't want to have anything to do with them. I had also made up my mind to never get pregnant again, and I had spoken to the Lord on this matter. That didn't make me sad. I was going to make the best of what I had all by myself for me and my children. I made sure I was working and could afford to support them and myself. Sometimes, I felt sorry for myself. I would talk to myself about the things I thought I couldn't change, but I was determined to make it in my life and show the world that I could do better all by myself. My children's fathers weren't in their lives and it did bother me, but I declared that what had happened to me wouldn't follow me and determine the life of my children. I gave them to the Lord when they were born, and so I took a stand over their lives.

Chapter 12
The Man, Noel

My journey wasn't easy, but it was worth it. I unapologetically owned my season of parenting, being single, healing, developing, growing and loving myself.

Little did I know back then that I was sharing my heart, healing and aspirations with my earthly angel, Noel. God bless him. He was my cheerleader from the sidelines. I could count on him every time. He was my best friend. One day, after so many years, he told me how he felt about me. I didn't know how to react or what to say. I could only giggle like a little girl.

I loved him back, but I was hiding my true feelings. First of all, he was my best friend. He showed me true and unconditional love. He had a way with words and when anything arose in my life, he knew how to calm me down and took away all the pains and trauma I suffered. He could easily take the bad feelings away from my mind. He knew how to make me laugh and wipe away my tears. He was a gentle giant full of love and compassion. He never allowed me to talk about my stepfather in front of him. He would say, "It takes away the beauty inside you, and it leaves you empty." I asked myself, "Where has he been all my life?"

He brought me experiences I never had before. When he touched my face, my body shivered and he would look deep into my eyes and his face would tremble. Still, he would just whisper a word of encouragement, tell me that all would be well, and that I should just have faith. A phrase he liked to say was, "What is not dead, don't throw it away." He was my life, but I still didn't know how to respond to his feelings. I wasn't getting any answers from myself!

We decided to keep our friendship going for a long time. We didn't want to jump into anything, and I was grateful because I wasn't ready to commit. I was afraid of any kind of relationship.

It took us five years to see each other in the same way. It just happened. He asked if I would come with him to see his mom and I looked at him in surprise "See your mom?" He said, "Yes, we are going to see my mom." That was when I knew he liked me in a different way a serious way. After planning the trip, we arrived in the parish of Saint Thomas where he was born. It was nerve wracking for me. I'm so glad it turned out great. His mom was so warm and welcoming. His sister embraced me as though we had known each other for a while. It was very easy for me to relax in their presence and feel at home.

It took another two years for us to become intimate with each other. He treated me like glass that would break if you weren't careful. He cared for me genuinely. We had many good times just talking, and I was able to be open and vulnerable for the first time. I was able to offload some of my burdens that I was carrying. I was happy for the first time in my life, and things were looking good. I could see a future with him. Eventually, I noticed that my body was changing. I was surprised to discover that I was pregnant. I think my body is too fertile. I felt unlucky about that before, but now I was elated. I was having a child with a man that I loved and was happy to be with. I told him that I was pregnant and he was supportive and kind. He looked into my eyes, rubbed my face, and smiled. We had come a long way from our friendship into this.

A Child Cries

After some months into my pregnancy, I was on my way to visit my daughter in Port Antonio. I decided to take a minivan. On the way, the van slid and went over the rails. I almost lost my life in that accident; however, my unborn child did. I lost my baby, and days later, I found out that it was a boy. That was the most devastating thing that could have happened to me. I contacted Noel, and he came to the hospital in Port Maria. I didn't know what to say. I didn't know how to communicate with anyone in those days. As a matter of fact, I didn't have any form of good communication skills at all, so discussing issues like losing the baby was hard for me. I went through the pain without talking about it. He didn't know how to break the ice so that we could talk about it. We tried to move past the accident and live our lives without talking about the pain we were both going through but it was hard on us.

I spoke to the Lord, and asked him, "What have I done to deserve all this pain and agony?" My cry for help was buried inside and went unnoticed. I didn't know what was going to happen to me after losing my son. I trusted in the Lord and cried out to him in my lowest moments. When the storm of life is raging over me, I abide in Him. The man I loved, and I were facing sad days. He couldn't find the words to comfort me or himself. I was in great distress seeing him grieving and suffering. It made my grief worse. I shut myself away and cried for the pain to go away and for a change to come into my life. He started visiting less frequently. When he came around, he caressed my face and looked deep into my eyes, but I couldn't read his thoughts or remove his pain. I understood his pain, but I couldn't do anything about it. The person I used to share my downfalls and misfortunes with was in pain because of me. I was at fault for the unfortunate condition we were in. I cried to God, "Where are you? Why me, Lord? Take the pain away."

Months had passed, and I was once again dealing with being by myself all over again.

God was listening when I prayed, and he decided to move on my behalf. The army was sending me to England for training. I went to visit my daughter and had a long conversation with her grandmother. I informed Ms. Morris of my decision to seize the opportunity and leave for training in England. She encouraged me to go. She said, "Go ahead. Go live, and don't die." With her encouragement, I decided to leave to train for special assignments. I was coming from nowhere without an education, but I was going to make it. God had favored me for a time such as this. I was ready for the change.

I was facing another challenge before I could leave. I had my four-year-old son, and I needed to talk to his father and see if he was willing to assist me in taking care of

A Child Cries

him for the time I was going to be away. I contacted him and he came over. We talked about it, but he refused to assist. He said he had a whole lot of issues and couldn't take his son. I was heartbroken, and left crying. This man was trying to stop me from claiming my blessing, and coming out of the gutter that I was in. I started crying out to the Lord for help, and He came through for me. I was not going to let this opportunity pass me by. I planned how to get my son's father to help me. I waited until two days before leaving, packed my son's bag, and wrote a list of things my son needed and what he couldn't eat and put them all together. I wrestled with myself as I cried ceaselessly until I built up the courage to do it. I couldn't take him to my mom because of my stepfather, and I didn't have anyone to help me. The pain I went through to do what I had to do broke me for weeks. I didn't have any other choice.

He came over to drop off the money, and I asked him again if he could watch his son. He refused again. I made up some excuse to go to the store, so I could leave the apartment. I told him that I would return, and asked him to watch his son until I came back. I went to the neighbors and asked her to tell him that I wasn't coming back. I had gone away, and he had to take my son home. I left him a letter telling him that all his son's things were packed. I cried as soon as I left. It was one of the most painful things

I ever had to do. My stuff was already at base because I needed to be there early in the morning. My heart was broken yet again. My neighbor accommodated me at her house until I had to report in. She was an elderly lady and she rocked me like a baby as I cried. She told me, "All is going to be well. The Lord takes care of His own." I accidentally ran into my son's father in the parking lot, and he tried to run me over, but God spared my life. He knew I had a purpose to fulfill. I told Noel that I was going away for a year to train, and he was a little disappointed even though he had been distant since I lost our child. I told myself that God knows our lives now and what they will be in the future. He makes his decisions based on his knowledge.

Chapter 13
New Chapter

I left the island of Jamaica to start my training not knowing what was ahead for me. I was open to new endeavors and experiences. I had never been outside of my country, and I wasn't prepared for the new life I was experiencing, but I was open to change for the better. I spent a year away upgrading my life and making better judgement calls for myself, such as, what I wanted to do with my life and where I wanted to go.

After a month, I tried calling my son's father to find out how my son was doing. I didn't get any answers from him. My heart hurt, and I missed my child. My daughter's grandmother made sure I was able to keep in touch with her. I tried calling my son's father multiple times, but I noticed I was blocked from calling him. I didn't speak with my son the whole year I was away.

When I got back to Jamaica, the first place I visited was where my son was staying. Upon my arrival at his aunt's house, I was greeted by his aunt. She spewed many harsh words letting me know that I was not welcomed there and that I should by no means come there again. The aunt told me that he said that I mustn't come to the house because I had left my child on the roadside and his family believed the lie. She didn't want to hear anything I had to say because I was wicked to leave my child. I was left weak and heartbroken. I called my 'friend' and son's godmother, who later turned out to be a foe rather than a friend, to assist me in this situation. The friend was plotting with my son's father because she wanted to have a relationship with him. I didn't find out about that until a few years later. That will be another chapter in another book.

I kept on going back to the house to see my child, and all my efforts seemed abortive. One day, I was walking up to the gate, and a beautiful, elderly lady came down to the gate and gave me the most beautiful smile imaginable. She said, "I am your son's great-grandmother." Her next words left me crying. "No one can stop you from being a mother. You are always going to be his mother. They can put this gate between you and him, but this cannot stop you from being his mother. Baby girl, your son isn't here. From the time you came back to now, his father boarded him out so you wouldn't get a chance to see him. But I promise you I will call you so you can get to see him and spend some time with him. Do you have a number?" I nodded and she continued, "Wipe your eyes and go home." I gave her the number to my mom's house and mine.

I left there even more heartbroken than before. Months passed and I still didn't hear from her. I thought about my son every day that passed. I did the best thing I knew how to do cry! It didn't make anything better, but it was comforting. I visited my daughter and spent time with her. Her grandmother welcomed me anytime and always made me feel at home. Portland was a place where I felt relaxed, and most like myself. I could also free my mind with some much-needed rest. Eventually, I had to go back home to Kingston. I had so much to face and a lot of decisions to make.

When I got home, I received a call from my eldest sister. She said that our sperm donor father had filed for her and my half brother from another woman, but not for me. That was another blow to my emotions and feelings, but I hid the pain as I normally did. Another waterworks episode, and another pain to bear. At the back of my mind, I needed to know if he was my real dad because I had heard repeatedly from my grandma that he wasn't. I shook the thought from my head and again, I dismissed the pain and carried on with my life. I still tried to get in touch with my son, but I still wasn't making any headway. His father had decided to block me because I wanted to do something meaningful with my life. There was a war raging in my life.

A cry for love. A cry for answers. A cry to find myself.

UNANSWERED QUESTIONS

"Mom, who is my dad?"

She looked at me quizzically. "What do you mean, who is your father?" I shouted at her, "I need answers to the question! "

She replied, "You know your father."

"So why does he treat me like I am not his own?" I knew it had to do with his mom, who never accepted me as his child because I wasn't born as light-complexioned as my sister. I laughed aloud. My mom stared at me like she thought I was going out of my mind. I asked her, "Who is Uncle Bob's father?"

She just stared at me not knowing where I was going.

New Chapter

"So, if Uncle Bob's my uncle, and they have the same father; why is he so black?"

She replied, "I don't know."

I walked away from her. I felt lost, and I still didn't have an answer. I just wanted to know why I was born. She knew that I was mad. I turned around, "Why didn't my so-called father file for me too?"

At that time, my mom had no idea what I was talking about.

I yelled, "She is going abroad, and I will be stuck here. Why me? Why me? Everyone hates me. Why was I born? Why did you bring me into this world? I am not wanted by anyone!" I ran out of my mom's house and went home to cry like always. All the pain of my life came crashing down, hitting me from the left and right. I cried when my brother and sister left the island. I felt rejected, alone engulfed with emptiness. I was in a place where there were no answers, but I lifted my faith in God to open a door for me. I couldn't bear anything more, but I must move on. I had to tackle the battle ahead of me. I was determined to find a way out of Jamaica. I wouldn't accept this oppressed lifestyle any longer. I went to pray to God asking him to help me. I left it all in his hands. I was moving on to seek other ways out of Jamaica.

A Child Cries

I decided to go visit the house again where my son was living, and to my surprise he was visiting from the boarding school that his father had placed him in. No one knew he was coming, so they didn't have time to hide him from me. His great-grandmother ushered me into the house quickly. She placed my son and I in a room and closed the door and told me to spend as much as I wanted with him. I was so grateful for the time that she allowed me to spend with my son. It was a task for me to leave because everyone was at home when I had to leave. His great-grandmother and I were trying to figure out a way to get me out of the house without anyone seeing me, so that she wasn't put into a compromising position. I didn't leave until very late in the night, but it was worth it for the extra time I got to spend with my son. I knew that his father had planned to have him disown me, but I made up my mind to be a mother to him no matter the outcome.

The next time I went to see him I brought my mom with me to see her grandchild, but he was taken away. Someone had told his dad that they saw me around there that night. His great-grandmother told me that they were fussing with her about letting me see him, so they took him away, and she had no idea where he was taken. She reminded me that I was always going to be his mother. I cried and left. I didn't know what to do. I opened my Bible and God took me to the book of Esther. Esther's story reminded me of the fate of evil Haman and how Esther rose to her calling and no longer lived a lie. Esther became a truly great person, and a woman of righteousness because evil Haman's plan had backfired.

I went to bed and woke up early. I prayed, prepared my mind to walk into my destiny, and went to the Canadian Embassy to try my luck. I didn't even know anyone in Canada. I didn't know the outcome either, but I had already placed God at the controls and willed myself to face this challenge with optimism. I was walking by faith and like Esther, I believe God would vindicate me.

At the embassy, I was standing in a queue and noticed that the lady at the helm was turning down everyone in front of me. As she was about to call me, I heard the voice of God saying, "Step out of the line." I looked around to see if someone was saying those words to me. I heard them again, "Step out of the line." I looked up, and the lady was about to call me. I felt like someone pushed me out of the line. The guy standing behind me walked in front of me towards the lady. Another window opened and the gentleman working there beckoned me to come on over. I walked up to him and greeted him with my biggest smile. All I had was the application in my hands. He asked, "Why do you want to go to Canada?" And out of nowhere, the words came out, "I am getting married." I don't know why I lied. Maybe it was my nerves? It helped my lie that the ring I always wore looked like an engagement type of ring.

He then asked, "Okay. Do you have a joint account with the person?"

I smiled and said, "Yes, I do."

He responded, "Okay. I need a copy of that account."

I nodded, and replied, "I will need to go and get it from the bank."

He gave me a stipulated time to return it. I called my Uncle Wayne, who worked at a bank not too far from the embassy. He added me to his account and told me not to move. He brought it to me, then stayed with me until the window opened again. That was it for me. I got a one-time entry visa. I told the Lord that it was all I needed. I was going to make the best of it from there on. I was going to help my children and my mom. God had been good to me, I couldn't complain, and so I didn't complain.

I now had something to look forward to. My life was about to be restored after all the ups and downs. I was leaving the army. My time expired and I wasn't signing up for another five years. I just needed a new beginning. My life had been like a roller coaster of wrong men, abuses, and lots of disappointments. I had cried so many tears. There were so many holes in my heart. I still struggled with the fact that I had lost my third child. I had been tossed about all my life. I had been homeless, my family walked all over me and treated me like an alien, my father disowned me and I felt disappointed with my life. I had never allowed my disappointments or negativities to affect me emotionally, but they still took a toll on my mental health. I remember when I was depressed and felt empty and lonely. During those times, I wanted a hug from my mom, but she didn't know how to show love and because of the challenges of her life, she had no love to give me. I understood her, though, and I never blamed or held her responsible for anything. In my eyes, she was controlled by a weak man and was a victim of her circumstances.

Tears rolled down my face. I felt like it was washing off all the heavy debris I had been carrying for a long time. I started to reflect on my younger years when I was deprived of food, clothing, and love. I had made a promise to myself that I was going to make it in life. I remember the numerous beatings I received for nothing, the isolation from my siblings, the childhood I never got to live, and the lonely days of being abandoned and rejected. The past scenes of my life were playing through my mind. I kept saying, "Thank you, Lord, for saving me from all the dangers that I have faced while I tried to live and stay safe from the unknown." I thought about the pain my mother would be in and how I wouldn't be able to protect her while I was away. But I had no choice. I needed to take advantage of this opportunity.

Before I left, I went to visit my mom to let her know of my departure. I was giving away my furniture and other belongings I had acquired throughout the years to my sisters. They didn't believe me when I told them that I was going away for good. Instead, they laughed at me. I had already made arrangements with my daughter's grandmother, and I also tried saying goodbye to my son. I had written him a letter that his great-grandmother had promised to read to him on my behalf. I had no more tears left to cry, so all I did was hug my siblings. I had nowhere to stay in Canada, I was walking by faith only. I had the little Canadian money I had exchanged and a note from a friend with the names of her aunt and uncle. Then, I was off.

In my heart I cried. I cried for my younger self. I cried for the little girl robbed of the love needed to feel safe and secure. I cried because I did not know how to console her, so I buried her deep in my heart and shut her away!

New Chapter

A SONG FOR MY MOM

I've had many tears and sorrows.
I've had questions for tomorrow.
There've been times, I didn't know
Right from wrong,
But in every situation
God gave me blessed consolation
That my trials come to only make me strong.

Through it all,
I've learned to trust in Jesus.
I've learned to trust in God.
Through it all,
I've learned to depend upon his word.

I've been to lots of places and
I've seen lots of faces.
There've been times I felt so all alone,
But in my lonely hours, yes,
Those lonely hours
Jesus let me know that I was his own.
I thank God for the mountains,
And I thank him for the valleys.
I thank him for the storms he brought
Me through.

Love you, Mama!

FROM ME TO YOU

You have fought a thousand battles, but you are still standing.
You have cried a thousand tears, but you are still smiling.
You have been broken, betrayed, abandoned, and rejected,
But you are still walking proud, you smile, you laugh,
And I am glad you live without fear.
You are beautiful inside and out.
You are humble and work hard.
And I love you.

Psalm 118:14 says, "The Lord is my strength and song, And He has become my salvation."

The battle is not yours, it's the Lord's. Your circumstances may bring darkness into your world, but as long as God is speaking to your spirit then your spirit will have the light that will shut down the darkness around you. When the light shines, darkness will flee, so in spite of what is happening in your five-sense realm, you can know in your mind that if God is for you, and who can be against you?

www.ingramcontent.com/pod-product-compliance
Lightning Source LLC
Chambersburg PA
CBHW071133090426
42736CB00012B/2114